GOD
first

D1547711

GOD
first

Setting life's priorities

BRYAN G. SIBLEY, M.D.

Acadian House
PUBLISHING
Lafayette, Louisiana

Library of Congress Cataloging-in-Publication Data

God first : setting life's priorities / by Bryan Sibley, M.D.
Lafayette, LA : Acadian House Publishing, 2016. | Includes
    index.
LCCN 2016038087 | ISBN 0925417637 (hardcover)
LCSH: Christian life. | Christian life--Methodist authors.
LCC BV4501.3 .S5757 2016 | DDC 248.4--dc23
        LC record available at https://lccn.loc.gov/2016038087

◆ Published by Acadian House Publishing, Lafayette,
  Louisiana (Edited by Trent Angers; editorial assistance
  by Darlene Smith; pre-press production by Charlotte Huggins)

◆ Cover design by Lauren Sibley, Sibley Designs,
  Lafayette, Louisiana.

◆ Printed by Sheridan Books, Chelsea, Michigan

Lessons from a journey of faith

Each of us is on a journey through life, and the journey is made richer, far richer, by the relationships we forge along the way. Though we may be born into very different circumstances, we each have an opportunity to learn life's lessons as we travel along.

And it's so important for us to pay attention to the teachable moments that come our way. It has been said many times, *"A moment of insight is worth a lifetime of experience."* I agree with this completely, and it applies well to Dr. Bryan Sibley's story. This book offers an opportunity to learn from him how a moment of insight can shape our thoughts and actions in ways we may never have imagined.

As I read the manuscript, I heard echoes of similar lessons I have picked up on my own Christian journey. One of those lessons is this: *"When you see a turtle sitting on top of a fence post, you know it didn't get there by itself."* Clearly, my friend Bryan understands this. For in the acknowledgements section of this book we see ample evidence of how others have influenced, guided and blessed Bryan's life. He knows that the journey is indeed enriched by the people with whom we travel, people who share God's grace with us.

All of us have lessons to learn, and Bryan makes it clear that he is no different. As you read this book you may recognize some of your own struggles and questions, as Bryan candidly shares his. These ten chapters offer several of the most important lessons any person of faith can learn. I commend each of these principles to you for implementation in your own faith journey.

Another life lesson this book recalls for me is this: *"People care how much the teacher knows once they know how much the teacher cares."* It's clear from the text in this book that Bryan Sibley is a teacher who truly cares – because of his love for Christ and the people Christ has called him to love.

As I read the chapter on gratitude, I could not help but think of how grateful I am to be both Bryan's pastor and his friend. I wholeheartedly recommend this book and what it teaches.

To God be the glory!

– *Rev. Richard H. Humphries*
Senior Pastor
Asbury United Methodist Church
Lafayette, Louisiana

Introduction

Doing God's will

Is it ever too early in life to begin one's journey of faith? My mom didn't think so, for on the day I was born she committed me to the service of the Lord. She wanted me to be a priest.

But there was a problem: I didn't "feel the call" until well after my young adulthood. And the call I felt was to the field of medicine and the care of children, so I became a pediatrician.

Now, I've always been active in the church. I grew up as a Roman Catholic then joined the United Methodist Church when I was about 30 years old. I wouldn't trade my upbringing and early adulthood in the Catholic Church for anything, for it is here that my relationship with Jesus not only began but took shape. What I learned has provided the basis on which my faith has grown, and that faith continues to be the port in the storms of my life.

In the mid-1990s, after a lot of prayer and soul-searching, my family and I joined Asbury United Methodist Church in Lafayette, Louisiana. Since then I've had the opportunity to be active in a wide variety of congregational activities - everything from international medical missions to the finance committee and a lot in between. In the summer of 2015, I was approved as a Certified Lay Minister in the Louisiana Conference of the United Methodist Church by Bishop Cynthia Fierro-Harvey.

While I'm not anywhere close to being a Catholic priest, it can be said that after some 50 years the faith of a young mother committing her infant son to the service of Jesus Christ may have finally borne some fruit!

Over the years, often in spite of myself, I've learned a few things, which are what prompted me to write this book:

- We, as Christians, are responsible for living our lives according to the way God has designed, equipped and intended us to live; in short, according to His will. This is so that we can do what it is He has created us to do in building His Kingdom and growing the Body of Christ.

- The only way any of us can do this effectively is through *a personal relationship with Jesus Christ – an active, personal relationship* which is developed and nurtured through prayer, Bible study, generosity, worship (both individual and community), ministry, service and personal witness.

Each of this book's chapters is devoted to a different aspect of life as a Christian. These are illustrated through a combination of Scripture and stories of my own journey of faith. It is my hope and prayer that this compact volume will be helpful to you as you seek to grow into who it is God intends for you to be.

– *Bryan G. Sibley, M.D.*

Contents

GOD
first

Come unto Me all ye that labor
and are heavy laden,
and I will give you rest.
(Matthew 11:28)

Chapter 1

God first, family second, everything else third

Don't be concerned about what to eat and what to drink. Don't worry about such things. These things dominate the thoughts of unbelievers all over the world, but your Father already knows your needs. Seek the Kingdom of God above all else, and he will give you everything you need. (Luke 12:29-31)

In the spring of the year 2000, I scheduled a meeting to visit with the Senior Pastor of my church to discuss what I considered some rather routine matters. But the outcome of that meeting proved to be anything but routine. And as a result, my life as a physician, a family man and a Christian was turned upside down, in a good way.

If ever I had any doubt about the truth of the old adage that God works in mysterious ways, that doubt has been laid to rest forever.

The meeting, which was to last only 15 minutes, was with Reverend Ed Boyd, the Senior Pastor of Asbury United Methodist Church, in my adopted hometown of Lafayette, Louisiana. The business at hand was to set a date for the baptism of my baby daughter, Blair, and to discuss ways to raise the money needed to fund a medical mission trip to South America.

I arrived at Ed's office at the appointed time and, in short order, he quickly answered the questions I had for him. After that, he was gracious enough to ask me to tell him about myself. And so I launched into a rather lengthy monologue about my life, background, hopes, dreams, plans, and opinions on the topics of the day. I digressed into how hard I was working at my job, usually 15 to 20 hours per day, in an effort to build my medical practice – all for the greater good of my family, of course.

I am sure he had a full calendar and more than a few other items on his agenda that day. However, he sat for a solid hour and a half and listened to my ramblings with what appeared to be great interest. When I finally paused to take a breath, he looked me squarely in the eyes and spoke up for the first time:

"God first, family second, everything else third."

During my self-absorbed, unrehearsed, and most likely unappreciated monologue, I had failed to ask him a single question. Therefore, his pronouncement caught me totally off-guard. Somewhat stunned, I was able to respond with only a single word:

What?

He laughed and then explained how he, too, early in his career, had become over-absorbed in his work. More and more, his work as a minister was keeping him away from his family. His circumstances had kept him from home so much that he needed to pause and re-focus his priorities, to re-examine how he was spending his time. That process of re-prioritizing his life led him to put God first in everything, he explained.

"Yeah, that's great. As soon as I get my practice to where I want it to be, I'll get to that," I replied.

Ed stopped me abruptly.

"No. You have to put God first in everything – every minute of every hour of every day – from the time you get up in the morning until you go to bed at night. After Him, your family must be your next priority, every minute of every hour of every day. If you do this, then God will take care of everything else."

I left his office that day a little stunned.

Until then it had never occurred to me to live my life as such. Up until that point I had been told, over and over, that hard work, self-reliance, self-determination, meticulous planning and intellect, if properly applied, would result in untold success. I had been trained in school, in residency, and in business to rely only on myself.

What Ed was telling me was completely contrary to everything I had been doing, and it simply did not make sense to me at the time.

Over the course of the next several weeks, Ed's words – "God first, family second, and everything else third" – continued to rattle around in my head. It was like a tune that got stuck in my mind.

I finally sat down and visited with my wife, Shelley,

about what I was experiencing: being torn between what our senior pastor advised me to do and what I had been trained to do my entire life. As she and I were talking about this dilemma, our oldest child, Lauren, who was nine years old at the time, walked in and overheard part of our conversation. She jumped right in.

"Dad, it's simple. Just look at the Ten Commandments – the first four are about God, the next one is about family, and the rest are about everything else," she said.

Ah, from the mouth of babes!

She proceeded to tell us that she had just learned this in her religion class at Our Lady of Fatima School, where she was in the fourth grade. As though Ed's comments hadn't bothered me enough, now my nine-year-old daughter's statements completely stopped me in my tracks. So I found our family Bible, dusted it off, and looked up the Ten Commandments.

Then God gave the people all these instructions:

ONE: *You shall have no other gods before Me.*

TWO: *You shall not make for yourself a carved image – any likeness of anything that is in heaven above, or that is in the earth beneath, or that is in the water under the earth.*

THREE: *You shall not take the name of the Lord your God in vain.*

FOUR: *Remember the Sabbath day, to keep it holy.*

FIVE: *Honor your father and your mother.*

SIX: *You shall not murder.*

SEVEN: *You shall not commit adultery.*

EIGHT: *You shall not steal.*

NINE: *You shall not bear false witness against your neighbor.*

TEN: *You shall not covet your neighbor's house; you shall not covet your neighbor's wife, nor his male servant, nor his female servant, nor his ox, nor his donkey, nor anything that is your neighbor's.* (Exodus 20:1-17)

How about that! There was the proof – right there in black and white – in God's Holy Bible: "God first, family second, everything else third."

It occurred to me at that very moment, as clear as day, that I had been prioritizing my life in an altogether different way: me first, me second, me third.

One night, a couple of weeks after my meeting with my pastor, I was sitting at my desk in my office. It was about 1 a.m. when a realization hit me: My oldest child was nine years old, and her time at home with Shelley and me was about half over. I had always worked extremely hard, and the harder I worked the less productive I seemed to be – and the more I was away from my family. Despite all of the training and education I had received on becoming successful, nothing I was doing seemed to be working.

At that moment, I made a conscious decision to "Just do it" – Thanks, Nike! – and trust God in everything. I went home, woke up Shelley, and told her I was not going to the office the next morning and would be spending the day at home. And that's exactly what I did.

Shelley, of course, expressed her opinion that I was finally cracking up.

Over the course of the next few days and weeks, I made a concerted effort to change the way I did everything, in accordance with what Ed recommended and the Bible commanded.

This radical, new approach began for me many years ago, in the year 2000. Now, I'll admit I certainly have not been perfect in this discipline. However, as I step back and review my life as it is now, compared to what it was before this re-prioritizing, I realize that my efforts to live in a way in which God is first in all that I do has borne some significant, positive results. Things have changed for the better, including these:

1. I used to worry about almost everything, e.g., making money, gaining weight, losing my hair, paying for our children's education, getting enough sleep, being treated fairly in my dealings with others, etc.

Now, though I still find myself feeling stressed from time to time (especially when I'm tired), I find that the grace of God has truly sustained me and that He has taken care of my family and everything else in my life.

2. I was rarely home, and when I was home I was usually either sleeping or cranky. Now, I can count on one hand how many of my children's activities I have missed. We have eaten most evening meals together, as a family. And my children have grown into the type of well-balanced young adults that can be only when God and family are top priorities in their lives.

3. It seemed that I used to never have enough money.

At that time, though we attended church regularly, I would usually drop only a few dollars in the collection plate as my offering to the church. Now, Shelley and I prioritize God in our finances, including the Biblical practice of tithing; and now, not only do we have enough money but we are also blessed to be able to share our resources – make that *God's resources* – with those in need.

4. In an effort to justify my old system of prioritizing, more often than not I reacted to others argumentatively. I seemed to be angry much of the time. Now, I find that I approach both personal and professional relationships by seeking God's perspective. My relationships are more fruitful and I find joy in almost all situations.

5. Because I was often worried and angry, I rarely slept well. Now, as I seek God's solutions to my problems (instead of my own solutions) I sleep much better, I feel better, I am easier to be around (I think), and I am much more productive in my daily life.

So, these are some of the blessings I've realized through re-prioritizing my own life. I know the Lord has so much more in store for you and me as we strive to put Him first in our lives!

Chapter 2

Serving the Lord
by serving others

*But among you it will be different. Those who are
the greatest among you should take the lowest rank,
and the leader should be like a servant. Who is more
important, the one who sits at the table or the one
who serves? The one who sits at the table, of course.
But not here! For I am among you as one who serves.*
(Luke 22:26-27)

I n the spring of 2000, I attended my cousin's
ordination into the Catholic priesthood. During the
Bishop's message to the newly ordained priests, he
reminded them that they were ordained to serve, not
to be served.

"This is the same wonderful message Christ gave to
His apostles 2000 years ago, and still gives to us today,"
the Bishop said.

A central theme of the Gospel has to do with service:
serving our friends, our communities, our families,
and even our enemies. This call is found not only in
the Bible, but also in our daily lives – through our
circumstances, our environments, and the people with
whom we interact.

In March of 1993, my wife, Shelley, and I were celebrating our fourth wedding anniversary at a restaurant in Houston. It was a very pleasant experience until, while enjoying our meal, I felt a tooth crack.

To complicate matters, we were in the process of moving from Houston to Lafayette, Louisiana, so I put off seeing a dentist until after we had moved.

Before the move, a couple of our friends hosted a going-away party for us. As a parting gift, these friends, who had grown up in Lafayette, gave us an address book filled with the names of local professionals, among them an insurance agent, a few lawyers, medical specialists, and providentially, a dentist.

I made an appointment with the dentist, Dr. Jim Nichols. Not only did he fix my tooth, but he and I also quickly became friends. It wasn't very long before he asked me to join him on a mission trip to Mexico, which I did.

I accompanied him on several of these trips and, four years later, he asked me if I'd be interested in going on a mission trip to Peru. After prayerful consideration, I agreed.

In preparing for the trip I solicited donations of medicines and supplies from other physicians, pharmacists and clinics in our community. One pharmacist called me and said he had many boxes of 800-mg ibuprofen tablets that he could no longer use, since smaller doses of the tablets were readily available without a prescription. He asked if I wanted them for the trip.

Typically, the medication needs for the mission trips I'd been on were in the categories of antibiotics, vitamins, and just about anything other than ibuprofen. I didn't expect to need ibuprofen, but since I didn't want to offend the pharmacist, I accepted his offer.

We packed the ibuprofen tablets into three large duffel bags, each weighing about 75 pounds, and hauled these bags, along with our luggage and medical equipment, through the airports in Lafayette, Dallas, Lima, Peru, and finally to our flight's destination, Moyobamba, Peru. From there, we strapped the duffel bags of ibuprofen and other baggage on top of a rented car for the eight-hour drive over the Andes Mountains, before we arrived at the foot of a river which is a tributary of the Amazon. We could travel no further in the car, so we loaded the duffel bags, along with the rest of our luggage, medication, tents, tools, equipment, food, and water onto small wooden motorboats for a four-hour journey down the river – at night.

Then we hiked about two miles into the jungle to our final destination, a remote village.

At each point of this journey, we complained about the weight of the bags, and I silently questioned if I was foolish for bringing this extra medication, given the likelihood that it would not be needed.

We arrived at the village at about 3 a.m. – 28 hours after leaving Lafayette. The other missionaries and I quickly pitched our tents and fell asleep.

Two hours later, we were awakened as the villagers

started moving around and began singing. Bleary-eyed and not speaking to each other much, we left our tents, ate a modest breakfast, enjoyed a great worship service, and then set up a makeshift clinic and started to see patients.

The first five or six villagers came to see us for help with some type of arthritis or muscle pain. I happily gave them some of our stockpile of ibuprofen. For the next four days, about 75 percent of the people seeking care actually requested help with some kind of physical ailment that could be easily treated with – You guessed it! – ibuprofen. As it turned out, ibuprofen was *exactly* what most of these villagers needed. Since we had brought so much, we were able to leave a six-months supply in the village.

In spite of the apparent divine intervention into this mission, I felt uneasy about it. Ibuprofen merely treats symptoms; this medicine is not a cure by any means. I felt that we had failed to provide a permanent cure for these people's ailments.

In response to my rather negative assessment, the lead missionary sat down with me and told me of how a calling he had felt led him to first venture into this jungle 18 months earlier. He then related how he was captured and held prisoner for three days by these same villagers, and how he witnessed to them about the saving grace of Our Lord. As part of his witness, he told them that if they accepted Jesus Christ as their Lord and Savior, God would abundantly bless them with, among other things, improved health and relief from pain. He continued:

"And just one and a half years later, here you are, a doctor from the United States, thousands of miles away, treating them and fulfilling my promise to them on behalf of Our Lord."

This missionary was saying in essence that he believed our actions were likely a fulfillment of God's promise to those Peruvian villagers.

God's call to serve is found not only in the Gospels, but also in our daily lives – through our circumstances, our environments, and the people with whom we interact. In the case of my trip to Peru, the way I see it is He called me by way of a cracked tooth, which led to a dentist, who invited me to the Amazon jungle to take ibuprofen to treat some ailing Peruvian people!

While this story is intended as a dramatic example of God's call to serve in my own life, I believe that, more often, we answer God's call to serve through our ordinary interactions with the people in our lives. Visiting a neighbor, shopping for a friend who is ill, helping someone by cutting his or her grass, sharing money or other resources with someone in need, inviting someone to church – these are all examples of our responses to God's call to serve as members of the body of Christ.

In conclusion, I challenge you to think about – and act upon – how it is that you can routinely serve Jesus Christ by serving your neighbor. Even if your act of service seems small, it may very well be an answer to that person's prayer.

Chapter 3

The Great Commission

*Then the eleven disciples left for Galilee, going to the
mountain where Jesus had told them to go. When
they saw him, they worshiped him — but some of
them doubted! Jesus came and told his disciples,
"I have been given all authority in heaven and on
earth. Therefore, go and make disciples of all the
nations, baptizing them in the name of the Father
and the Son and the Holy Spirit. Teach these new
disciples to obey all the commands I have given you.
And be sure of this: I am with you always, even to
the end of the age." (Matthew 28:16-20)*

I n the period between Jesus' resurrection from the
dead and His ascension into Heaven, He instructed
His apostles to spread His teachings to the far corners
of the Earth. This directive is known throughout
Christendom as The Great Commission.

Jesus' wishes in this regard are as clear today as they
were back then, in 33 A.D. Consequently, I believe
the future of Christianity depends on two kinds of
people: those who are willing to continue to follow
Jesus' instructions and those who are open to receiving the message.

It is common knowledge that membership in

Christian churches today is declining in the U.S. and Europe. There are likely several reasons for this phenomenon, such as the passing away of older members, lack of a sense of fulfillment in being a member of a church, and the increasing busyness of life. Whatever the reason, it appears that more and more Americans seem to think that organized religion is irrelevant in their lives.

While in the process of becoming a Certified Lay Minister, I had the opportunity to spend a couple of years preaching and leading worship at the Port Barre United Methodist Church, in Port Barre, La. Part of the preparation for my first sermon involved researching the history of this small congregation, and I was inspired by the diligence of the founder. According to the official history of the congregation, in 1908 the original pastor, who traveled by train, would make regular stops in the town and would hold services in a tent set up in a field next to the train depot. A moveable pump organ would be brought into the tent for music. The tent was blown down in 1909 and was too damp and moldy to bother raising again.

Services were then held in a schoolhouse on the banks of Bayou Teche until the number of people attending the services made the schoolhouse too crowded. The congregation then began meeting in a room in back of a saloon.

In 1912, the church organized a Sunday School program; services were held on the first floor of the saloon, while Sunday School classes were held in its upper room. The size of the congregation kept growing, so a church building was constructed in 1919. The building was expanded in 1951. In 1971, the congregation held its first service in a new, larger church.

These founders, and countless others involved in the church's formation, were the embodiment of The Great Commission in a very real way. Two important players were evident back in the early days of forming churches throughout America: those making disciples of others and those becoming disciples. Both of these roles are pivotal in the flourishing of churches, and because of this – and the work of the Holy Spirit – the churches grew.

*   *   *   *   *

In John's Gospel, we read that the risen Lord appeared to the apostles on multiple occasions; however, Thomas was not with the group during the first apparition.

One of the twelve disciples, Thomas (nicknamed the Twin) was not with the others when Jesus came. They told him, "We have seen the Lord!"

But he replied, "I won't believe it unless I see the nail wounds in his hands, put my fingers into them, and place my hand into the wound in his side."

Eight days later the disciples were together again, and this time Thomas was with them. The doors were locked; but suddenly, as before, Jesus was standing among them. "Peace be with you," he said. Then he said to Thomas, "Put your finger here, and look at my hands. Put your hand into the wound in my side. Don't be faithless any longer. Believe!"

"My Lord and my God!" Thomas exclaimed.

Then Jesus told him, "You believe because you have seen me. Blessed are those who believe without seeing me." (John 20:24-29)

Even though these disciples had lived and worked with Jesus for three years of His public ministry, and even though they were clearly instructed to go out and make disciples of all the nations, apparently they still needed to see Jesus in a resurrected state to strengthen their belief in Him as the Messiah and to further motivate them to carry on His work on Earth.

Today, the rates of crime, drug use, gambling and pornography, among other things, are higher than ever. People seem to be pursuing these vices more than ever before in an effort to find some level of happiness, joy, comfort or relief that is missing from their everyday lives. Christians know that true happiness, joy, comfort and relief can be found through a personal relationship with Jesus Christ.

But it often takes someone to share a word, an experience, or an invitation with another person in order for such a relationship to begin. Too often we in today's church see only the reasons why we cannot be that person to invite another to learn about Jesus. Sure, it can be difficult to overcome the excuses and to shift from being a believer who says, "I will do that some day ..." to one who stands in awe at the power of Jesus Christ and is motivated to action by that awe. The task, however, is doable.

The majority of Americans are Christians, which is to say that we have accepted Jesus as our Savior; yet many people still need someone to help them become engaged with their faith – to show them they are loved, to encourage them, to befriend them, to invite them to church.

I encourage you to become that someone. You don't have to be a public speaker, a leader of a large church or chairman of a church committee. Just invite someone to church.

Many of us know someone who may be in need of such an invitation. By simply inviting and bringing others to church, we are accepting and living out The Great Commission – just as Jesus instructed.

Chapter 4

Tithe, because it all belongs to God anyway.

The earth is the Lord's, and everything in it. The world and all its people belong to him. (Psalm 24:1)

"Bring all the tithes into the storehouse so there will be enough food in my Temple. If you do," says the Lord of Heaven's Armies, "I will open the windows of heaven for you. I will pour out a blessing so great you won't have enough room to take it in! Try it! Put me to the test!

"Your crops will be abundant, for I will guard them from insects and disease. Your grapes will not fall from the vine before they are ripe...." (Malachi 3:10-11)

The practice of tithing is one that seems to have lost its luster among many mainstream churches today. This may, at least in part, explain the declining church attendance in the United States.

The discussion of money in church is a conversation that tends to cause people to tune out, stop listening, and/or develop anxiety or even anger. However, the Bible is very clear about God's view of money: It all belongs to Him, He has given it to us for us to use, and we are to return a portion to Him.

33

Let's examine a few key points about money and financial management by looking at what the Bible has to say about these topics – and how we are to interpret the relevant passages.

Throughout history people have debated whether or not the Bible should be read and understood literally or figuratively. For example, in Matthew 5:29 we read, "So if your eye – even your good eye – causes you to lust, gouge it out and throw it away. It is better for you to lose one part of your body than for your whole body to be thrown into hell." I think most of us believe this is a figurative instruction, not a literal one. On the other hand, consider the reading from Malachi: "Bring all the tithes into the storehouse so there will be enough food in My temple. If you do," says the Lord of Heaven's Armies, "I will open up the windows of heaven for you. I will pour out a blessing so great you won't have enough room to take it in!" This passage can be read as literal instructions for people living in Old Testament times as well as for the generations who occupy the Earth today.

Regardless of how you choose to interpret the Bible – literally or figuratively – I think we all ultimately agree that its content represents the Word of God, our Creator, Redeemer and Savior. Because of this, we as Christians can reasonably be expected to apply the Bible's wisdom to our lives in every aspect, including our finances.

Let's look closely at the word "tithe." Biblical scholars,

pastors, priests, rabbis and others agree that "tithe" means to give 10 percent to support the church. Many of us have approached this idea thinking, *Ten percent? That's one out of every ten dollars! Does that mean that every time I get ten dollars, I am supposed to give one to the church? Is that before or after taxes? Is that on my gross or my net income?*

The short answer is "yes."

Wow! you may be thinking, *I can't make ends meet now. How am I supposed to make it if I'm giving away ten percent of my income to the church?*

For many years, my wife Shelley and I struggled with the practical aspects of tithing. That is, we were not sure how to do it. You see, my income is somewhat variable. Typically, in a general pediatrician's office we tend to be busier during the winter and not so busy during the summer. As a result, we usually receive more money during the fall and winter than we do during the rest of the year. This requires that we be careful to save for a rainy day, so to speak. Early in our marriage, we put money in the collection plate every time we attended church. It was at about that time in my life when I heard a story that has stayed with me ever since. It goes like this:

There was a guy who came to church with his family. As they were driving home afterwards, he was complaining about everything about the service. "The music was too loud. The sermon was too long. The announcements were unclear. The building was hot.

The people were unfriendly." He went on and on, complaining about virtually everything. Finally, his very observant son said, "Dad, you've got to admit it wasn't a bad show for just a dollar."

This story really hit home for me. It gave me a sudden awareness of my responsibility to give more of what I earned back to the church. I started writing a check to the church on a regular basis. While our giving did increase, I still was not giving a full ten percent of my income – primarily because I was concerned that if I gave that much I would not have enough left to pay our bills and to live in the manner we sought to live.

At about that time, I attended a presentation at our church which was sponsored by the Louisiana Methodist Foundation. It was on planned giving and, as part of the talk, the speaker pointed out that there was a fairly easy way for people with variable incomes to tithe.

"Look at the adjusted gross income on your tax return last year, move the decimal point over one space; take that number and divide it by 12; and finally take that number and give it to the church every month for the upcoming year," he explained.

Tithing Formula for People with Variable Income:
Adjusted Annual Gross Income divided by 12 (months per year) = Monthly Income

Monthly Income x 10% = Amount of Monthly Tithe

That was an "Ah-ha!" moment for me. I had never really thought about it that way, but this was a simple formula for calculating my tithe. Furthermore, I believe this was a clear, divine message demonstrating for me how simple it would be for my family to tithe. I took it as such, and since that day in 2005, Shelley and I have used this formula.

At some point in my walk of faith, it occurred to me that God is happy to multiply resources and blessings for those who practice tithing. I believe that one reason for this – besides the fact that tithing is an act of faith – is that the church (and the work of the church) is the direct beneficiary of such blessings.

Shelley and I accepted and acted upon the Lord's challenge to tithe, as it is written in Malachi. What we've experienced is just what God has promised: Our financial situation has improved, and this gives us the ability to share without hesistation. And, believe me, we are grateful for this each and every day.

This last point – having resources to help those in need – really should be the focus of this chapter. I believe this is the heart of God's purpose for the tithe. It is plain to see that there are those among us who are in need. The church, the Body of Christ on Earth, must have resources available to help when these needs arise. It seems to me that if every adult member of the church tithed ten percent of his or her income, then the church would have more than enough resources to help the needy.

Ultimately, tithing is an outward manifestation of an inward desire to put God first in our lives in all that we do. As mentioned earlier, the process of making God's will our top priority – followed by our families, and then everything else – is a way of prioritizing by faith.

* * * * *

Many mainstream churches in the United States are clearly in decline, and a lack of funds is at least part of the reason for this. It's interesting to note, however, that many non-mainstream "mega-churches" are growing and thriving and seem to be flush with money. Those churches, it seems, have created a culture of responsibility for its members, and one of those responsibilities is tithing.

Why, then are so many of us so uncomfortable about this aspect of our faith?

In 2011, Shelley and I agreed to co-chair a $3.5 million debt-elimination campaign at our church. During that campaign, we often heard detractors comment about the perception that "All the church wants is my money." Now, the consultant with whom we were working – Joe Park of Horizons Stewardship – suggested we reply to such a negative comment with these words:

"That's not true; we also want your prayers, your presence, service, and witness; we want *all* of you!"

I think this is how God feels about us, too. He wants *all* of us, all of the time, in a loving, abiding, relationship with Him. It seems that many of us are more comfortable being in a relationship with God by way of our prayers or our church attendance or our service, or occasionally our witness, but not so much with our money. But we were not designed or created to be in a partial relationship with the Lord. No, in fact, He gave His Son completely and totally so that we can enjoy a complete and total relationship with Him.

God gave us free will, but He also gave us a set of rules and instructions that we can freely choose to follow. When we use this free will to live our lives walking by faith, in accordance with God's rules, abiding in Him, we find that giving ten percent back to God is a truly joyous practice. It is also a means by which we can fully experience the God-filled life we have been created to live.

Chapter 5

It's crystal clear:
We are to care for the poor

But when the Son of Man comes in his glory, and all the angels with him, then he will sit upon his glorious throne. All the nations will be gathered in his presence, and he will separate the people as a shepherd separates the sheep from the goats. He will place the sheep at his right hand and the goats at his left.

Then the King will say to those on his right, "Come, you who are blessed by my Father, inherit the Kingdom prepared for you from the creation of the world. For I was hungry, and you fed me. I was thirsty, and you gave me a drink. I was a stranger, and you invited me into your home. I was naked, and you gave me clothing. I was sick, and you cared for me. I was in prison, and you visited me."

Then these righteous ones will reply, "Lord, when did we ever see you hungry and feed you? Or thirsty and give you something to drink? Or a stranger and show you hospitality? Or naked and give you clothing? When did we ever see you sick or in prison and visit you?"

And the King will say, "I tell you the truth, when you did it to one of the least of these my brothers and sisters, you were doing it to me!" (Matthew 25:31-40)

T he Bible contains more than just a passing commentary about the importance of God's charge to His people to care for the poor. In fact, the word "poor" is mentioned more than 200 times in the Scriptures.

Here are a few examples:

• "In a lawsuit, you must not deny justice to the poor." (Exodus 23:6)

• "It is the same with your grape crops: Do not strip every last bunch of grapes from the vines and do not pick up the grapes that fall to the ground. Leave them for the poor and foreigners living among you." (Leviticus 19:10)

• "Give generously to the poor, not grudgingly, for the Lord your God will bless you in everything you do." (Deuteronomy 15:10)

• "...Oh, the joys of those who are kind to the poor! The Lord rescues them when they are in trouble." (Psalm 41:1)

• "Give justice to the poor and the orphan; uphold the rights of the oppressed and the destitute." (Psalm 82:3)

• "Those who oppress the poor insult their Maker, but helping the poor honors Him." (Proverbs 14:31)

• "If you help the poor, you are lending to the Lord – and He will repay you!" (Proverbs 19:17)

• "John replied, 'If you have two shirts, give one to the poor. If you have food, share it with those who are hungry.'" (Luke 3:11)

• "'Instead, invite the poor, the crippled, the lame,

and the blind.'" (Luke 14:13)

* * * * *

In January of 2003, my family and I had just moved back to Lafayette, Louisiana, from Houston. We were still living out of boxes. My staff and I were moving into my new office. I was essentially starting over, having just left a job in Houston where I was the medical director of a small children's rehabilitation hospital.

I was struggling with the idea of whether I should participate in the Louisiana Medicaid program. Around that time, this program – which mainly provides Federally funded, State-managed health insurance for those with low incomes – had undergone significant changes in the way it was being operated. The bulk of these changes had to do with more strictly managing the care of Louisiana's poor, including limiting access to emergency room care for non-emergent visits and decreasing the amounts paid to physicians for their services. (Payments to physicians from the Medicaid program were and are significantly lower than what we receive from private insurance companies.) Because of this, the conventional wisdom of many of my colleagues was to stay as far away from the Medicaid program as possible.

In my previous practice, I had not participated in the Medicaid program. I was working 20-hour days, had become distant from my family, and ended up financially distressed. Since Medicaid reimbursement to physicians is lower, you can imagine the dread I felt over the prospect of getting paid less for the services we would be providing.

A majority of children in Louisiana are enrolled in the Medicaid program, and historically they have had diminished access to care. So, I saw that I had the opportunity to provide better care to this needy population and potentially do more good for these children than I ever had.

As I prayerfully struggled with this decision, I was unpacking boxes in my new Lafayette office. I came across a book written by Larry Myers entitled *Hungry for God: Are the Poor Really Unspiritual?* Larry is a minister and missionary who created Mexico Ministries when he was in his early forties. He did this in response to a calling he felt from God and did so in spite of his church's leadership telling him they could not support him because their rules did not allow pastors to become missionaries after the age of forty.

Larry had given me a copy of the book several years earlier but I had never read it. Since this was the first time I had come across it in some years, I set it aside with plans to start reading it very soon. Later that day, still thinking about whether to participate in the Medicaid program, I sat down with Larry's book and was able to read through it in short order. Imagine my surprise when I read the last sentence:

"I join with the apostles and appeal to you: Remember the poor."

Well, the events leading up to my finding and reading that book, especially the closing sentence, were the answer to my prayers. I decided right then and there not only to participate in the Medicaid program as a provider, but also to become involved in the leadership, management, and on-going evolution of this program as it existed in Louisiana at the time.

Since that day, I have enjoyed the practice of pediatrics in a way greater than I ever thought I could. I have had far fewer administrative headaches due to the Medicaid program than I had feared. My patients and their families have continued to express their gratitude for the care they receive through my practice. My family life is richer than it has ever been. I have not been able to fully count the multitude of blessings I have received as a result of this decision.

My patient population is not limited only to those enrolled in the Medicaid program. Our doors are open to virtually anyone who wants to come into the office. On a few occasions, colleagues have asked me how I handle the inevitable question from a privately insured patient's mother about "the others" in the waiting room who don't appear to be as financially blessed. My response:

"We provide the same level of care to all children, regardless of how much money their parents make, and if anyone is not happy about that, they are welcome to seek care elsewhere."

It's been a surprisingly interesting and very rewarding experience to have worked with the poor for more than half my career.

I've learned that people are more often alike than they are different, regardless of their socioeconomic status.

I've learned that people all need Jesus, regardless of their station in life.

I've learned that Jesus has called each of us to live according to His will. I believe He expects us to do our part in being the living Body of Christ on this earth by loving and serving Him and others in all that we do – regardless of their socioeconomic status and ours.

And I've learned that we're always, always to take care of the poor.

Chapter 6

God's superior plan for us

*That is why I tell you not to worry about everyday
life – whether you have enough food and drink, or
enough clothes to wear. Isn't life more than food,
and your body more than clothing? Look at the birds.
They don't plant or harvest or store food in barns,
for your heavenly Father feeds them. And aren't you
far more valuable to him than they are? Can all your
worries add a single moment to your life?*

*And why worry about your clothing? Look at the
lilies of the field and how they grow. They don't
work or make their clothing, yet Solomon in all his
glory was not dressed as beautifully as they are. And
if God cares so wonderfully for wildflowers that are
here today and thrown into the fire tomorrow, he
will certainly care for you. Why do you have so little
faith?*

*So don't worry about these things, saying, "What
will we eat? What will we drink? What will we
wear?" These things dominate the thoughts of
unbelievers, but your heavenly Father already knows
all your needs. Seek the Kingdom of God above
all else, and live righteously, and he will give you
everything you need.*

*So don't worry about tomorrow, for tomorrow will
bring its own worries. Today's trouble is enough for
today.* (Matthew 6:25-34)

I am a planner. I like to plan. Though I do not like to admit it, I probably like to plan just for the sake of planning.

I'm not sure why I am wired this way, but for as long as I can remember I have planned things. For example, when I was six years old I asked my dad if I could take some money from my savings account because I was planning a surprise party for Mom's upcoming birthday.

As a middle school student, I remember planning to be a pediatrician, remaining single until I was 35 years old and then finding a wife. As it turned out, I met my wife, Shelley, when we were 20 years old and we were married when we were 23. At that time, I remember planning to have our first child when we were 27 years old. It turned out that our daughter, Lauren, was born when we were 25.

Scripture tells us that God says, "I know the plans I have for you, plans to prosper you and not to harm you, plans to give you hope and a future." (Jeremiah 29:11, New International Version). I think we can all agree that God's divine plan for our life has, is, and will always be the best plan there is.

We may know this intellectually, but do we know it in our gut? Do we know it in our soul? Do we live our lives as though we believe it? I wish I could tell you that I always do. I mean, I try to, and I am better at it than I used to be, but I still have a long way to go.

Why is this? Why is it that we know that our God,

the Lord of the Universe – who loves us infinitely and who has great plans for us, who seeks to prosper us, who has our best interest at heart – has a plan for us and yet we can't seem to trust in Him or His plan?

Is it "human nature" or something else? Is it a lack of faith?

In Exodus 16:4-5, we read:

"Then the Lord said to Moses, 'Look, I'm going to rain down food from heaven for you. Each day the people can go out and pick up as much food as they need for that day. I will test them in this to see whether or not they will follow my instructions. On the sixth day they will gather food, and when they prepare it, there will be twice as much as usual.'"

Later in that same chapter (Exodus 16:15-20) we read:

"And Moses told them, 'It is the food the Lord has given you to eat. These are the Lord's instructions: Each household should gather as much as it needs. Pick up two quarts for each person in your tent.'

"So the people of Israel did as they were told. Some gathered a lot, some only a little. But when they measured it out, everyone had just enough. Those who gathered a lot had nothing left over, and those who gathered only a little had enough. Each family had just what it needed.

"Then Moses told them, 'Do not keep any of it until morning.' But some of them didn't listen and kept some of it until morning, but by then it was full of maggots and had a terrible smell. Moses was very angry with them."

Based on this story, it would appear that our desire to plan for the future according to our own understanding (rather than trusting in the Lord's plan) pre-dates all of us by a lot more than just a few generations. I suspect that people have always been fearful of the unknown, the future, what lies ahead for them. Because of this, we tend to resort to our own devices in an effort to secure our own promising outcomes. When we live this way, I wonder how many of us miss out on the best of what God has to offer.

In Proverbs 3:5-6 we are told, "Trust in the Lord with all of your heart and lean not on your own understanding; in all of your ways, submit to Him and He will make your paths straight." (New International Version) I believe the reason God tells us to live our lives by placing our trust in Him is because He knows that if we follow His direction and His plan, rather than our own, the benefits (both secular and eternal) – to our lives and to those with whom we interact – will be immeasurable.

One practical method of living this life of faith is simply to accept that Jesus Christ is the Son of God, who came to this earth, lived among us, and died for the forgiveness of our sins, and who offers eternal salvation to those who believe in Him. Once we accept this, our future is secure: We know where our earthly journey ends, and since our destination is certain, it is nonsensical and a waste of time to consume our lives with endless planning and worrying.

Rather, it is much wiser to utilize our days serving the Lord by serving others. This typically means that while we should plan our days, we should create these plans with the knowledge that our circumstances may change and that such changes may be opportunities to better serve God. When we approach life in this manner, we will experience far less stress and enjoy the blessings that come with trusting in the Lord.

* * * * *

The wisdom of trusting in God's plan shines through in a story that my aunt Deborah tells. It took place in a Lafayette, La., hospital when Aunt Deborah's sister, my Aunt Cleo, was laid up in the Intensive Care Unit with a life-threatening medical condition. Both of these ladies are my mother's sisters.

Aunt Deborah tells it this way:

"I was teaching English as a second language in St. Martin Parish schools and had unexpectedly finished early for the day. I was sitting in my car with nowhere in particular to be, and I started praying that God would use me and direct my path.

"About that time, a relative called me and told me that my sister Cleo was in surgery, so I decided to go on to the hospital about noon. I think all of Cleo's kids were there except for her youngest son, Peter. He wasn't expected to come in at that point as the surgery was expected to be routine to repair the place where a previous surgery had failed.

"But at one point after that second surgery, Cleo's son Jeff came into the waiting room and was crying. He said it didn't look good. Shortly after that, all of the family members who were in the waiting room were told we could go in and see her for a few minutes. We knew it would be to say good-bye.

"When I saw Cleo she was extremely swollen and was hooked up to life-support. I asked her daughter Connie if it would be all right if I prayed for her, and she was happy that I wanted to do that. I knelt at the foot of Cleo's hospital bed and started praying. People were coming and going, but I couldn't stop praying. I couldn't get up off my knees. It felt like a spiritual force was keeping me there. I noticed that while I was praying, Cleo's vital signs were showing that she may have had a chance to live. When I stopped, the numbers would drop. I continued praying. I asked Connie if she wanted me to leave so the immediate family could have time with Cleo alone. She said she wanted me to continue praying.

"Cleo's husband was extremely distraught. He looked at me at one point, after about an hour of my praying, and through his heartache and tears he said, 'Deb, if you can bring her back, I'll give you anything you want.' At that point my heart was breaking for him. I told him, 'I have no power to bring her back. But I know Jesus does, so I'm just asking Him. He has the final say.' I was thinking the whole time about King David asking

God to heal his dying son, and his thinking that as long as the boy was still alive he was going to keep asking God for his life. That's what I was doing for my sister.

"I stayed there at the foot of Cleo's bed until the nurse began telling us to go home. That was about 10:30 p.m. Everyone left but me. I begged to be able to stay, and the nurse granted me 15 more minutes. Then 15 more. Then 15 more. I pulled a stool to the end of Cleo's bed and was sitting there holding onto one of her feet. My faith for her survival was definitely larger than a mustard seed! I was convinced God would grant her more life.

"As I was praying, just above a whisper, I heard a man's voice in the hallway outside of the ICU. He said, 'I'm here to see my mother.' It was Peter, the youngest of Cleo's five children. He'd been driving all day from central Texas to get to the hospital.

"We talked for a while. At that point Cleo was totally unrecognizable due to the swelling from kidney failure. Peter and I had a last look at her, then we went home.

"The next morning, I received a call that Cleo had passed away during the night. After the funeral, Peter came and hugged me and said, 'Thank you so much for being there. I'm glad I didn't have to be alone when I saw her like that.'

"We learned that Cleo had died only about an hour after Peter and I left – after I'd stopped praying.

"That's the longest prayer vigil I'd ever kept. My knees were sore, and I was losing my voice, but I knew

I had to keep praying. God could have kept her alive without my prayers, of course. Prayers aren't magic. But they do have the power to touch the heart of God, to incline His ear toward His children. In His kindness and compassion, God kept a mother alive long enough for her son to see her before He called her home."

* * * * *

I once heard it said that we should apply insight to our lives, which means that we should plan wisely, make our needs known to God and those around us, then proceed in faith as God provides what we need. Is this not the wisdom demonstrated in the story of the Israelites in the desert, of the apostles in the Book of Acts, of the change of my Aunt Deborah's plans?

Many of the greatest disappointments I have experienced have occurred because I chose to follow my own plans at all costs – at the expense of following God's plan. On the other hand, when I have chosen to "Let go and let God," my journey has been joyous and I have experienced contentment, surprise, relief, and ultimately a closer relationship with my Creator.

I challenge you to seek the Lord in all you do, especially in those circumstances outside of your control. By doing this, you will not only enjoy the bountiful blessings God has planned for you, but also be a conduit of God's blessings to others in your life.

Chapter 7

Expect miracles

The leader of a synagogue came and knelt before Jesus. "My daughter has just died," he said, "but you can bring her back to life again if you just come and lay your hand on her."

So Jesus and his disciples got up and went with him. Just then a woman who had suffered for twelve years with constant bleeding came up behind him. She touched the fringe of his robe, for she thought, If I can just touch his robe, I will be healed.

Jesus turned around, and when he saw her he said, "Daughter, be encouraged! Your faith has made you well." And the woman was healed at that moment.

When Jesus arrived at the official's home, he saw the noisy crowd and heard the funeral music. "Get out!" he told them. "The girl isn't dead; she's only asleep." But the crowd laughed at him. After the crowd was put outside, however, Jesus went in and took the girl by the hand, and she stood up! The report of this miracle swept through the entire countryside. (Matthew 9:18-26)

One definition of the word "miracle," according to the *Merriam-Webster* Dictionary, is "a surprising and welcome event that is not explicable by natural or scientific laws and is considered to be divine." Neither this nor any other definition I have found included the phrase, "having occurred in the Bible."

I mention this because it seems that many people in today's world doubt the existence of miracles. While we are happy to accept the biblical accounts of God using Moses to part the Red Sea and Jesus raising Lazarus from the dead, we are often reluctant to believe that miracles do occur in our world today.

Is this because we live in a time and place during which so much seems to be wrong with humanity? Is it because we look around and we do not see the "Moseses" of our day? Is it because we are so busy with our own lives that we fail to notice God working in and around us?

In searching for the answers to these questions, it is important to focus on at least two facets the Scripture shown at the beginning of this chapter: the characters (the leader of the synagogue and the woman with the hemorrhage) and what they had in common, namely, faith.

In Hebrews 11:1, we read, "Faith is the confidence that what we hope for will actually happen; it gives us assurance about things we cannot see." The biblical characters to whom I refer at the beginning of this chapter indeed believed that what they hoped for could and would happen. And it did! They were not all that different from us, were they? After all, many of us still have concerns about how we are going to earn enough income to meet our family's needs, how we will receive adequate treatment for illnesses and disease, etc. Perhaps what we do not have is "the confidence that what we hope for will actually happen."

Please understand that I am not saying that if we just have a little more faith, then we will prosper and be healed and that life will be a bowl of cherries. However, I am saying that, just as God was in biblical times, He is alive and active today. He is aware of our circumstances. He loves us and He answers us and responds to our faithfulness.

*　*　*　*　*

Shortly after I started my pediatrics practice in 1993, I had the opportunity to treat a six-months-old baby who was brought into the emergency room in total organ system failure. Essentially, he was dying. This infant had suddenly become ill at home and his parents had brought him to the emergency room. I happened to be on call.

The baby was admitted to the pediatric intensive care unit and placed on full cardiorespiratory support. We were preparing to transfer the child to a hospital in New Orleans for a higher level of care when the parents asked if their pastor could come into the unit and pray for the baby. He was brought in and he, the parents, the nurses, and I gathered around the baby's bed and prayed.

The baby was transferred to the hospital in New

Orleans later that night. I fully anticipated a phone call from the physician in New Orleans to tell me the baby did not make it.

The next morning, that physician did call but instead he asked me why I had transferred this healthy baby to his intensive care unit. I asked him to clarify and he told me that shortly after arrival in New Orleans the baby suddenly became better, life-support was withdrawn, and within a few hours this infant was taking a bottle and acting normally!

In 1997 I was on that mission trip to Peru which I mentioned earlier in the book. We were in the middle of the Amazon jungle. On the second day we were there, I was going about the business of seeing patients in a hot, makeshift clinic located in a hut in a tiny village.

A mother brought one of her children to see me because the child had a cough. He was about nine years old, and during the examination I noticed that he was blind. His mother told me, through two interpreters (the local, native dialect translated to Spanish, and then Spanish to English), that she thought he lost his sight when, as a baby, he had experienced a very high fever. He had been unable to see ever since that time.

One of the other missionaries was an optometrist. That day he was working with the building crew on erecting a small chapel for the village. I sent one of my assistants to get him so he could examine the boy's eyes. A few minutes later he came into the clinic, performed his exam and confirmed that the child was indeed blind.

I evaluated the boy, gave him some medicine for the cough, and was about to send him away when one of the college students on the trip asked if we could pray for him. Naturally, I said "yes" and that young college student led the prayer while we all laid hands on the boy. After we prayed, the boy walked away into the crowd of people who were in the clinic.

A few minutes later, the optometrist, who was standing nearby drinking a cup of water, said to me:

"Bryan, get that kid."

"Which one?" I asked, as there were so many in the room.

"The one we prayed for," he replied.

After some searching we found him.

"Give him something," the optometrist said.

"What?" I asked, a little puzzled.

"Hand him something, anything," he reiterated.

I reached into my backpack and pulled out a pack of cookies, I held it up to this child, and he reached for it, with a smile that I will never forget. It was obvious that his sight had been restored!

A few years later I was seeing a five-year-old girl in my office. She was accompanied by her grandmother, who reported that the child had awakened that morning and had not been acting normally. This report is a very common one in a pediatrician's office and usually it does not amount to much.

In this case, however, this child had a severe, life-threatening case of bacterial meningitis. She was admitted to the pediatric intensive care unit. Within a few hours she had significantly worsened to the point of requiring a ventilator to breathe, and her brain had swollen to a degree that it was clear her life was in danger. This was in spite of the fact that all appropriate medical interventions had been initiated immediately.

Later that day, about eight hours after this ordeal had begun, I contacted a neurosurgeon and a pediatric intensive care specialist about her rapidly deteriorating condition, and they agreed that she would likely not survive. With a heavy heart, I walked into her room in the pediatric ICU to break the news to her parents.

As I walked in, I saw the child's grandmother on her knees next to the child's bed praying fervently. I decided not to interrupt her but took the opportunity to examine the child once more. What I found was that her pupils, which had been fixed and dilated all day long, were beginning to react to light. I immediately repeated the scan of her brain which revealed a reversal of the brain swelling. By the following morning, this little girl no longer required the mechanical ventilator and, several days later, she walked out of the hospital without any problems.

I share these stories, not because I think I had anything to do with these children's outcomes, but because they were surprising and welcome events that were not explainable by any natural or scientific laws – the very definition of miracles. Further, I report these stories because I believe the outcomes to be divine in nature. I also believe that one explanation for these miracles, simply put, is the faith of the people involved.

In all three cases, I personally witnessed an unwavering faith in the power of God – by a set of parents, a college student, and a grandmother. Their faith in a loving God and His Son, Jesus Christ, was what not only prompted them to pray but it also sustained them through trying experiences and the subsequent miraculous conclusions to those experiences.

* * * * *

I attended a retreat in early 2012 and it included a powerful prayer service in the chapel. At the end of the service, as the retreat attendees stood up from the pews and turned around to exit, we noticed a banner which had been placed in the back of the chapel for our benefit. It read, "Expect miracles."

Our natural secular cynicism teaches us the opposite. The "wisdom" of the world teaches us to expect misery, debt, disappointment, failure and heartache. But I choose to believe in a totally different reality – the Word of God as it is found in the pages of sacred scripture.

Because of this – and because of what I have seen with my own eyes – I do expect miracles!

Chapter 8

Walking by faith, not by sight

"You don't have enough faith," Jesus told them. "I tell you the truth, if you had faith even as small as a mustard seed, you could say to this mountain, 'Move from here to there,' and it would move. Nothing would be impossible." (Matthew 17:20

I believe in Divine Appointments: those times, places and meetings that have been ordained by God and that are designed to impact our lives and the lives of those with whom we come in contact.

But, I don't think we always know when we've arrived at such places and times. It may not be until days, months or years later that we realize that some event in our lives was, in fact, a Divine Appointment. On the other hand, unfortunately, we may never realize it.

In any case, if we are to be on time for these appointments, it requires that we walk by faith and not by sight. I suspect that being guided by faith is not a disposition with which most of us are born. If you're like me, you like to see the road in front of you before you take a step, and you want to know what's on the agenda before agreeing to a meeting.

One of the very interesting things about being human is the free will that God gives us. It is the power and freedom to choose what we will do in any situation. We often use this gift to attempt to predetermine our path in life, and to tightly control the outcomes of our activities, both major and minor. But God wants us to use this free will to trust in Him, to trust that He has our best interest at heart. That is, he wants us to walk in faith. What's so reassuring about this is that when we choose to be guided by faith, what we often find is an outcome that is far superior to what we ever would have dreamed of on our own!

In 1979, as a high school freshman, one of my teachers was a bit of a local legend in the small town where I grew up. Richard Pizzolatto, affectionately known as "Coach Pizz," had coached just about every high school team sport there was. By the time I started high school, he had stopped coaching but was still teaching American history and civics. It was in my civics class that I had the opportunity to meet him. Over the years he had, in a sense, "adopted" several of us high school students, serving not only as a mentor but also as an additional father-figure in our lives. I accepted an invitation to one of his famous pasta and meatball meals, and he and I became fast friends. Since that time so many years ago, our relationship has evolved into the closest of friendships. We have relied on one another for advice, care, companionship and support during the many peaks and valleys of our lives. I continue to be blessed by his advice, humor, generous spirit, and dogged determination.

In 1984, during my second year of college, I was sitting in a microbiology class one day and the professor made an announcement that a friend of his, a dermatologist, was looking for a college student to work in a part-time position in his office as a medical assistant.

I wasn't looking for a job and my parents had told me they would prefer that I not work while in school, but there was something about this announcement that prompted me to approach the teacher after class and ask about the job. Then I called the physician's office and got an appointment with him and his office manager the very next day. They told me that the job required that I arrive at the office most weekdays at about 6:15 a.m. to open the office, work until class began, then return to the office after class until closing time at about 5:30 or 6 p.m.

As I considered this offer, I realized that my days would suddenly change from 4- to 6-hour days to more than 12-hour days. Nevertheless, something prompted me to press on, and I accepted the job.

This turned out to be one of the best decisions of my life. As a result of my taking the job, the physician, Dr. James "Ronnie" Bergeron, became one of my greatest mentors; I learned more about dermatology from him than I did during the remainder of my medical education. And I obtained firsthand experience about the practice of medicine that has served me in untold ways throughout my career.

In 2001, I was at a point in my career where I felt like I needed a change. I had been praying about what it was that God wanted from me, where it was that He wanted me to go, and how He'd have me get there. About that time, one of my colleagues called out of the blue and told me about a position in Houston that he thought would be perfect for me. It was an opportunity to serve as the medical director of a small children's hospital that was designed to provide rehabilitative and transitional care services to children who had survived catastrophic illnesses and injuries.

Again, I felt something nudging me forward, so I applied for the position and ultimately accepted it. In the process of making this transition from my practice in Lafayette, La., my family and I faced a number of challenges, such as selling our house, closing my practice, and finding new schools for our children, a new home and a new church.

We weren't sure how we'd meet these challenges, but the Lord provided. Our house sold, my practice was successfully transitioned, we found a good school for our children, we joined a fantastic church, and we found a conveniently located townhome to rent while we looked for a new house.

About 18 months later, my family became a little homesick and we decided to return to Lafayette. However, before we left Houston, the owners of the hospital where I was working offered me a position doing some consulting work with the families of children with special healthcare needs; it was a position that did not require me to live in Houston. After more than 10 years, I'm still doing that consulting work.

As I look back on this particular part of my life, I realize I never planned any of these key, pivotal events: the dinner invitation from my high school teacher, my college professor announcing a job opportunity that led to a great relationship with a mentor, and a colleague calling me about a job in a field that has become a large part of my life's work. I truly believe each of these events were Divine Appointments. These were experiences of faith; I believe they demonstrate that when we actively trust God, He will provide for us in ways we could never have imagined.

God knows what we need more than we do, and He loves us infinitely in a way that is beyond our comprehension. He tells us that there is no need to worry. He promises us that when we walk by faith and not by sight we will find that the outcome is so much better than if we do it the other way around.

Yet, in spite of this, we still find it hard to walk by faith.

Why is this?

Why can't we take what we know to be true in our hearts and minds and apply it in our lives?

As I searched for answers to these questions, it occurred to me that they may lie in common experiences that resonate with most of us: learning to swim or ride a bicycle, for instance. Think back to your childhood, when, step by step, an important, loving adult in your life took you on a journey which that adult knew was important to your future. Each step of the way you really couldn't see what was ahead; you probably worried about falling off the bicycle or sinking in the pool. Yet, in spite of your fears, the adult was there encouraging you and asking you to trust him or her. Little by little, you took the next steps, gained a little more trust, accomplished a bit more – and before you knew it, you were cycling or swimming without help or injury!

I believe this is similar to the way God sees us in our own walks of faith. We're His children whom He loves, and because of this love He continues to encourage us to take the next step of faith, gain a little more trust, and accomplish a bit more. And before we know it, we're living the life He has planned for us!

Chapter 9

Forgive as you wish to be forgiven

"In keeping with your magnificent, unfailing love, please pardon the sins of this people, just as you have forgiven them ever since they left Egypt." Then the Lord said, "I will pardon them as you have requested." (Numbers 14:19-20)

Then Peter came to him and asked, "Lord, how often should I forgive someone who sins against me? Seven times?"

"No, not seven times," Jesus replied, "but seventy times seven!" (Matthew 18:21-22)

A pparently there are not only a lot of people who are interested in the subject of forgiveness, but a tremendous amount of thought has been put in on the topic.

I did a Google search of the word "forgiveness" and found 55,700,000 results; a search on Amazon.com turned up 14,271 different books on the subject.

Definitions of the word "forgive" include these: to cease to blame or hold resentment against someone or something; to grant pardon for a mistake, wrongdoing, etc.; to free or pardon someone from penalty.

I'm sure we all know someone who is so nice, so generous, so grateful, so kind-hearted, and so forgiving that he or she has no enemies. Albeit rare, these folks do exist.

However, I must confess that I'm not one of them.

I guess the problem I have is that I want to be right, all the time, and I want everyone else to know that I'm right.

In spite of this particular personality defect, however, I don't like anyone to be mad or upset with me, or to be in a disharmonious relationship with me.

To live life completely without strife is virtually impossible, but we can make strides toward this goal if we are willing to forgive and to be forgiven. I have had to find a way to deal with an occasional lack of harmony in my relationships, and that way, at least in part, is by giving and receiving forgiveness.

* * * * *

In Luke's gospel (15:11-32), we read the parable of the prodigal son, which Jesus related.

"A man had two sons. The younger son told his father, 'I want my share of your estate now before you die.' So his father agreed to divide his wealth between his sons.

"A few days later, this younger son packed all his belongings and moved to a distant land, and there he wasted all his money in wild living. About the time his money ran out, a great famine swept over the land, and he began to starve. He persuaded a local farmer to hire him, and the man sent him into his fields to feed the pigs. The young man became so hungry that even the pods he was feeding the pigs looked good to him. But no one gave him anything.

"When he finally came to his senses, he said to himself, 'At home even the hired servants have food enough to spare, and here I am dying of hunger! I will go home to my father and say, "Father, I have sinned against both heaven and you, and I am no longer worthy of being called your son. Please take me on as a hired servant."'

"So he returned home to his father. And while he was still a long way off, his father saw him coming. Filled with love and compassion, he ran to his son, embraced him, and kissed him. His son said to him, 'Father, I have sinned against both heaven and you, and I am no longer worthy of being called your son.'

"But his father said to the servants, 'Quick! Bring the finest robe in the house and put it on him. Get a ring for his finger and sandals for his feet. And kill the calf we have been fattening. We must celebrate with a feast, for this son of mine was dead and has now returned to life. He was lost, but now he is found.' So the party began.

"Meanwhile, the older son was in the fields working. When he returned home, he heard music and dancing in the house, and he asked one of the servants what was going on. 'Your brother is back,' he was told, 'and your father has killed the fattened calf. We are celebrating because of his safe return.'

"The older brother was angry and wouldn't go in. His father came out and begged him, but he replied, 'All these years I've slaved for you and never once refused to do a single thing you told me to. And in all that time you never gave me even one young goat for a feast with my friends. Yet when this son of yours comes back after squandering your money on prostitutes, you celebrate by killing the fattened calf!'

"His father said to him, 'Look, dear son, you have always stayed by me, and everything I have is yours. We had to celebrate this happy day. For your brother was dead and has come back to life! He was lost, but now he is found!'"

In this story we see the reconciliation and the deepening of relationships that occur when forgiveness is given and when forgiveness is received: The father in the story is hurt by his son's leaving and squandering his inheritance, but his relationship with his son is restored when he puts his son's sins in the past and offers forgiveness. The son's relationship with the father is restored when he returns to the father with his hat in his hand, so to speak, and asks for then receives and accepts the father's forgiveness. The family is restored when their perspective on this situation is changed because of the father's explanation: "For your brother was dead and has come back to life! He was lost, but now he is found!"

Isn't this our story? Haven't we all done something in a relationship that resulted in an unanticipated outcome that damaged the relationship? These experiences occur every day among couples, family members, coworkers, church members, teammates, business partners, and others in a variety of relationships.

In order for these relationships to be restored, both parties have to find a way to put the incident behind them and then extend, and receive, forgiveness.

*   *   *   *   *

Years ago, I found myself unintentionally looking for mistakes in the work of others, especially among the hospital nurses with whom I had to work. I am ashamed to admit it, but I spent so much time and energy pointing out these mistakes and problems among the nurses that I became unproductive and unhappy in my daily life.

I'm sure the nurses weren't happy either.

At the time, I told myself that what I was doing was in the best interest of improving patient care. You know, pointing out the faults of the nurses, taking them to task over these faults, spending time in discussions with their supervisors – all in an effort to "make them better nurses."

Of course, the end result was that the nurses didn't like me. (Read, they despised me.) However, they did, in a sense, change the way they practiced: They refused to take my patients because they didn't want to work with me! This led to my becoming resentful and not wanting to work with them either.

I am sharing this because I believe it illustrates what can happen when we stubbornly hold fast to our beliefs, do not consider other perspectives, disregard the feelings of others, fail to take responsibility for our given situation, and just focus on circumstances rather than on solutions – in short, when we fail to forgive.

It took a fair amount of "in your face" constructive criticism by people closest to me – my wife, my employer, my partners, my pastor – for me to realize that it was my approach, not the quality or character of the nurses, that was the problem. However, by this time, my frustration and aggravation were so ingrained that all I felt was resentment, anger, and blame (kind of like the prodigal son's brother). After all, I had done "nothing wrong," yet my relationships with all of these people were terrible.

In order to improve these relationships, I found that I had to do the following:

1. Ask the Lord for forgiveness.
2. Let go of any feelings I had about my "being right," i.e., self-righteousness.
3. Seek forgiveness from those I had offended.
4. Accept forgiveness from those who offered it.
5. Begin to reconcile.

Because of these steps and the tremendous character of the nurses involved, I believe that my relationships with the vast majority of these wonderful people, indeed, have been restored and hopefully enhanced.

The process of reconciliation can be tricky. I was once told, "Just because you forgive or have been forgiven, that doesn't mean that trust is automatically restored or that either person in the relationship is required to trust the other again."

As I thought about this statement and the process of forgiveness and reconciliation, I realized that it is certainly possible (and even likely) that many of us can forgive but not ever be reconciled with the other.

I think it's important to remember that while we should forgive as we have been forgiven (by Christ), forgiveness should not necessarily be the end point of the healing process between people. I've come to believe that reconciliation is probably the greater goal, and forgiveness is an important step toward that goal.

Now, I am not advocating continuing in a relationship that can cause harm, but I am suggesting that those who are estranged because of a problem or conflict in the past should at least seek to find common ground between one another. For once both parties have exchanged forgiveness and have chosen to focus on the mutually acceptable aspects of their relationship, I believe that the processes of healing, trusting and seeing the good in the other begins. Once this happens we are well on our way to reconciled relationships.

In Luke 23:34 we read that, while hanging on the cross, Jesus said, "Father, forgive them, for they don't know what they are doing."

This is really good news for us! Even though we approach forgiveness and reconciliation in our crude and imperfect ways, because of the life, death and resurrection of Jesus Christ, the work of forgiveness of our sins and reconciliation between God and humankind has already been perfected on our behalf.

Chapter 10

Be relentless in expressing gratitude

Rejoice always, pray continually, give thanks in all circumstances, for this is God's Will for you in Christ Jesus. (1 Thessalonians 5:16-18) (New International Version)

T he first time I read this directive in Paul's Letters to the Thessalonians, I began immediately to practice it in my own life. I was surprised how easy it was to "rejoice always, pray continually, and give thanks in all circumstances" - that is, until the worship service ended and I had to leave the sanctuary!

Some theologians refer to the edicts in this passage as the "standing orders" for Christians - you know, those methods of behaving as God would have us behave, no matter what. Most of what I've read about this passage focuses on the first two orders: "rejoice always" and "pray continually." However, I'd like to focus on the third: "give thanks in all circumstances."

This passage doesn't say "give thanks only when things are going well" or "be appreciative when someone does something nice for you" or "give thanks only on Sundays and Thanksgiving Day." No, in fact Paul is clear that God wants us to give thanks at all times, in all places, no matter what.

By the way, you'll also note that it doesn't say, "give thanks *for* all circumstances."

Paul is telling us that, because of what Christ has accomplished on the cross – the supreme sacrifice that enables our eternal salvation – there is no circumstance in which we cannot find something for which to be grateful.

Paul was very familiar with the concept and the practice of giving thanks. He spent a fair amount of his ministry as a prisoner, and he chose to be grateful more *in* his circumstances than *for* his circumstances. He was in jail and, I suspect, he wasn't necessarily grateful for his imprisonment, but during that time he was grateful for the opportunity to continue to preach and to bring people to know Jesus.

If we allow it to be, can't this also be our story?

If you're like me, you've probably had experiences that didn't seem fair or at least weren't circumstances you'd have chosen. For instance, an unexpected illness, bills that couldn't be paid, an unbudgeted expense (home or auto repair), the loss of a loved one, loss of a job, etc. Aren't these the "prisons" of our own lives, the "iron bars" that hold us back from doing what we want to do?

I think it's important to consider that while these unfortunate circumstances keep us from satisfying our wants and desires, they just might be allowing us to serve our God in a way that is greater than we ever could've imagined – just like the apostle Paul, while he was imprisoned.

Like Paul, we always have something for which we can give thanks!

When the negative circumstances in my life pile up, I make a conscious effort to remind myself of some of the many blessings I've received:

• I have a wonderful wife to whom I've been happily married since 1989, and our three children are healthy, successful and well-balanced.

• I am a member of a church in which people are engaged in its mission and where people are supportive of one another and our community at large.

• I have the privilege of serving our patients; they seem to enjoy the relationship we have and they demonstrate their gratitude for the care we provide.

The main point here is that no matter what our situation in life, we always have something for which we can be grateful.

For many, the question is how do we actually "give thanks"?

Does this mean that we tell God "thank you"?

Does it mean we tell others "thank you"?

Does it mean that we should focus on God and His blessings in our lives rather than allowing ourselves to be overwhelmed by our current circumstances?

Does it mean that we should use our God-given talents to demonstrate our love for God by serving others?

Does it mean that in spite of whatever situation we find ourselves in we should act politely, with integrity and with a positive attitude?

I believe the answer to all of these questions is "yes"!

Consider these five simple ways for expressing gratitude:

1. Make time to visit with those people in your life whom you appreciate.

2. Tell people that you appreciate them and what they do for you.

3. Write a thank you note.

4. Listen to others when they are talking to you.

5. Pray for those to whom you are grateful.

Aside from the supplies necessary to write and mail a note, none of these expressions of gratitude costs anything. Yet, by practicing them on a regular basis you may find your life to be much more in line with what God has planned for it.

Epilogue

On sharing the Good News

"For this is how God loved the world: He gave His one and only Son, so that everyone who believes in him will not perish but have eternal life. (John 3:16)

One of them, an expert in religious law, tried to trap him with this question: "Teacher, which is the most important commandment in the law of Moses?" Jesus replied, "You must love the Lord your God with all your heart, all your soul, and all your mind. This is the first and greatest commandment. A second is equally important: Love your neighbor as yourself. The entire law and all the demands of the prophets are based on these two commandments."
(Matthew 22:35-40)

I have often wondered how this book would impact the lives of those who read it. As I was writing, I asked myself a number of questions:

Will readers incorporate these lessons into their daily lives?

Will they use this information to make an impact on the lives of others?

Will this material be helpful to people as they seek to grow the Kingdom of God?

In attempting to answer these questions, it occurred to me that none of the lessons contained herein can ever achieve their full potential unless the reader has a personal relationship with Jesus Christ. In other words, if we have not accepted Jesus Christ as our personal Lord and Savior, we can never fully realize the benefits of these lessons.

God sent His Son, Jesus Christ, to the earth for a number of reasons: so that we can know Him more personally, live into the potential for which He has created us, and, ultimately, spend eternity with Him.

The essence of Jesus' response to the question about the greatest commandments is simply that we are to love God and to love others. The relevant question for us all is this: If loving God and loving others is such a simple concept, why aren't we better at it?

I believe one answer is that we, as Christians, have a tendency to get so caught up in our own brand of Christianity that we miss Jesus' point about loving others; and in the process we have been losing the battle for souls. That is, we have been so focused on defending our own view of Christianity that perhaps we have become self-righteous and stand-offish toward others who don't share our vision and our practices entirely. And in doing so, we very likely are turning others off – and away from Christ – rather than drawing them to Him.

It seems to me that, by hiding behind our traditions, our personal perspectives and our own preconceived notions of who belongs in God's Kingdom, we are inadvertently excluding people who are different from us:

- People whose skin color is different
- People of a different socioeconomic status
- People who have achieved different educational levels
- People who have different sexual orientations

We seem to forget that God, through Jesus, has already made the decision about inclusion: He includes everyone! Therefore, we are called to live lives in such a way that we do all we can to offer Jesus Christ to everyone!

As we all know, there is an awful lot of suffering, pain, turmoil, discord and dissatisfaction in our world today. People are dying because they need a Savior. It is as though they are starving amidst a great abundance of food or dying of thirst while standing in the middle of a fresh spring of water. They suffer because they do not know how to – or they refuse to – access the bounty all around them.

This is where we come in.

I am convinced that we, just like so many before us, are the keys to building the Kingdom of God. And we do this by sharing the Good News that Jesus Christ came to this earth, as God in the flesh, to show us how we are to live, so we can be saved and help others toward the same goal of salvation.

I hope that the lessons which I've shared in this book will help us all live into our faith in a way that people are not only attracted to us but also seek to know more about us and our God. These lessons, you see, are all about being free to live according to God's will, free to live by placing Him first in all we do, and free to live by sharing the Good News of Jesus Christ with everyone He sends our way.

In closing, I pray that God will bless you abundantly and, in doing so, will show you how to incorporate these lessons into your daily life so that you can become all that He has created, equipped and intended for you to be. I pray all of this in Jesus' Most Holy Name, Amen.

Index

Note: The Scriptural passages referenced
in the text begin this index.

Acknowledgements

This book would not have been possible without God's grace and a growing relationship with Jesus through the power and strength of the Holy Spirit. Nor would it have been possible without the inspiration, support and prayers of so many people in my life. These include, but certainly are not limited to, the following:

• Shelley, my wife and best friend, my closest advisor and confidant, who always seems to know exactly what's best for us, both individually and as a family.

• Our children, Lauren, Garrett and Blair – all of them wonderful, supportive and well- balanced.

• Trent Brasseaux, our daughter Lauren's fiancé, who has been a real inspiration by demonstrating patience, persistence, and a positive attitude through an inordinate number of obstacles in his young life.

• My parents, Scott Sibley and Cheryl Turner, who instilled in me a basic love of Jesus and devotion to His church throughout my life.

• Richard Pizzolatto (a.k.a. "Coach Pizz"), who has lived his life demonstrating the unconditional love, friendship and mentorship that could have come only from the Lord.

• Kelley and Paul Sobiesk, our best friends whom we met through what I know was a Divine Appointment and without whom we would have lost our sanity years ago.

• Dr. James Ronald Bergeron, for his patience and willingness to show me what it means to be a caring husband, father, leader, servant and physician.

• Dr. Jim Nichols, who has been not only a great friend and a wonderful dentist but also a living example of how we should use our God-given talents to serve His people, especially the poor, around the world.

• Rev. Ed Boyd, for serving as God's messenger in so many ways, especially in telling me to prioritize my life by putting God first, family second, and everything else third.

• Rev. Dick Humphries, my brother in Christ who has gone above and beyond the call of duty in helping me identify and pursue God's call on my life.

• Jeigh and Mark Stipe, good neighbors who not only read and critiqued my manuscript but also helped me to find a publisher.

• Elie Tabchouri, a good friend and confidant who walks the walk of a true Christian.

• Mike Craton, my loyal friend and advisor whose unwavering presence at weekly breakfasts has made my life so much better.

• Becky Link, the sister I never had, who has been kind enough to listen to me rant every other week for more than 20 years.

• Carl Groh, who is widely known as a gifted artist and who is also a gifted, often silent, servant of Christ. His service to his community and his friendship have taught me much about building God's Kingdom.

• Peggy and the late Bill Rosson, my in-laws, who have demonstrated the type of unconditional love of which Jesus spoke in the Scriptures.

• The congregations of Asbury and Port Barre United Methodist Churches, who have allowed me to serve them and who have propped me up in spite of my shortcomings.

•My Aunt Deborah Shelton, for her humor, encouragement and willingness to share her story in this book.

•My able staff, our patients, all the nurses and other healthcare professionals with whom I've had the privilege of working over many years.

• Matt Lafleur and my niece, Erin Rosson, for their help with the editing of this book.

About the Author...

BRYAN G. SIBLEY, M.D., is a pediatrician who practices in Lafayette, Louisiana, and a Certified Lay Minister in the Louisiana Conference of the United Methodist Church.

The 2013-17 president of the Louisiana Chapter of the American Academy of Pediatrics, he devotes much of his practice to the care of children with special healthcare needs. He is a clinical instructor at the LSU School of Medicine in New Orleans and past Chief of Pediatrics at Lafayette General Medical Center.

His medical training and his church affiliation have taken him on a number of medical mission trips to Mexico and Peru.

Dr. Sibley has served his church – Asbury United Methodist Church – as a lay leader, liturgist, Sunday school teacher and member of the worship and finance committees. He was named the 2016 chair of the St. Thomas More Catholic High School Strategic Planning Committe, and is a past chair of the school's Advisory Council.

An active public speaker, he gives presentations to a wide variety of professional, civic, community and church organizations.

He is married to Shelley (*nee* Rosson) Sibley, and they have three children.

Suggested Readings

The Prayer of Jabez: Breaking Through to the Blessed Life
by Bruce Wilkinson

Heaven is for Real: A Little Boy's Astounding Story of His Trip to Heaven and Back by Lynn Vincent and Todd Burpo

To Heaven and Back: A Doctor's Extraordinary Account of Her Death, Heaven, Angels, and Life Again (A True Story) by Mary C. Neal, M.D.

Seeing Gray in a World of Black and White: Thoughts on Religion, Morality, and Politics by Adam Hamilton

Making Sense of the Bible: Rediscovering the Power of Scripture Today by Adam Hamilton

Enough: Discovering Joy through Simplicity and Generosity
by Adam Hamilton

Not Your Parents' Offering Plate: A New Vision for Financial Stewardship by J. Clif Christopher

Momentum for Life: Sustaining Personal Health, Integrity, and Strategic Focus as a Leader by Michael Slaughter

Interrupted: When Jesus Wrecks Your Comfortable Christianity
by Jen Hatmaker

The Generosity Factor: Discover the Joy of Giving Your Time, Talent, and Treasure by Ken Blanchard

Same Kind of Different as Me: A Modern-Day Slave, an International Art Dealer, and the Unlikely Woman Who Bound Them Together by Ron Hall and Denver Moore

Halftime: Changing Your Game Plan from Success to Significance by Bob Buford

Inspiring Books
from
Acadian House Publishing

God First
Setting Life's Priorities
A 96-page hardcover book that encourages persons of faith to set priorities, starting with "God first, family second, and everything else third." The book has 10 chapters, with themes that center on gratitude, care for the poor, forgiveness, trusting in God's providence, etc. The chapters are anchored in Scripture and illustrated with inspiring stories from the author's faith journey. (Author: Bryan G. Sibley, M.D. ISBN 0-925417-88-2. Price $14.00)

Dying In God's Hands
A 152-page hardcover book that provides keen insights into the hearts and minds of the dying. It is based on interviews with terminally ill hospice patients, in which they share their hopes, dreams, fears and needs. The interviews provide evidence that faith in God and belief in the hereafter are the greatest strengths of the dying. Designed to comfort the dying and their loved ones. (Author: Camille Pavy Claibourne, APRN. ISBN: 0-925417-64-5. Price: $16.95)

Purses & Shoes For Sale
The Joys and Challenges of Caring for Elderly Parents
A 216-page hardcover book about the author's journey as a caregiver to her elderly parents in the twilight of their lives. Packed with suggestions on how to deal with issues encountered by adult children of the elderly. Includes Q&A, practical advice, useful websites and glossary of terms. (Author: Camille Pavy Claibourne, APRN. ISBN: 0-925417-96-3. Price: $17.95)

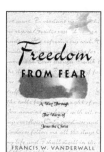

Freedom From Fear
A Way Through The Ways of Jesus The Christ

Everyone at one time or another feels fear, guilt, worry and shame. But when these emotions get out of control they can enslave a person, literally taking over his or her life. In this 142-page softcover book, the author suggests the way out of this bondage is prayer, meditation and faith in God and His promise of salvation. The author points to parables in the Gospels as Jesus' antidote to fears of various kinds. (Author: Francis Vanderwall. ISBN: 0-925417-34-3. Price: $14.95)

Getting Over the 4 Hurdles of Life

A 160-page hardcover book that shows us ways to get past the obstacles, or hurdles, that block our path to success, happiness and peace of mind. Four of the most common hurdles are "I can't / You can't," past failures or fear of failure, handicaps, and lack of self-knowledge. This inspiring book – by one of the top motivational speakers in the U.S. – is brought to life by intriguing stories of people who overcame life's hurdles. (Author: Coach Dale Brown. ISBN: 0-925417-72-6. Price: $17.95)

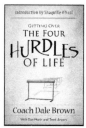

Waiting For Eli
A Father's Journey from Fear to Faith

A 176-page hardcover book about a Lafayette, La., couple and their infant son Eli who was born with a dreaded birth defect called *spina bifida*. It is an inspiring story of faith, hope and the power of prayer. The book has a strong pro-life, pro-love message, and is made even more compelling by the author's descriptions of little miracles along the way. (Author: Chad Judice. ISBN: 0-925417-65-3. Price: $16.95)

TO ORDER, list the books you wish to purchase along with the corresponding cost of each. Add $4 per book for shipping & handling. Louisiana residents add 9% tax to the cost of the books. Mail your order and check or credit card authorization (VISA/MC/AmEx) to: Acadian House Publishing, Dept. B-81, P.O. Box 52247, Lafayette, LA 70505. Or call (800) 850-8851. To order online, go to www.acadianhouse.com.